T0397999

My Body, My Rules

I USE MY VOICE

BY THERESA EMMINIZER

Enslow PUBLISHING

Please visit our website, www.enslow.com.
For a free color catalog of all our high-quality books, call toll free
1-800-398-2504 or fax 1-877-980-4454.

Library of Congress Cataloging-in-Publication Data

Names: Emminizer, Theresa, author.
Title: I use my voice / Theresa Emminizer.
Description: [Buffalo] : Enslow Publishing, [2025] | Series: My body, my
   rules | Includes bibliographical references and index. | Audience:
   Grades K-1
Identifiers: LCCN 2023053904 (print) | LCCN 2023053905 (ebook) | ISBN
   9781978539440 (library binding) | ISBN 9781978539433 (paperback) | ISBN
   9781978539457 (ebook)
Subjects: LCSH: Assertiveness in children–Juvenile literature. |
   Assertiveness (Psychology)–Juvenile literature.
Classification: LCC BF723.A74 E46 2025 (print) | LCC BF723.A74 (ebook) |
   DDC 158.2–dc23/eng/20231220
LC record available at https://lccn.loc.gov/2023053904
LC ebook record available at https://lccn.loc.gov/2023053905

Published in 2025 by
Enslow Publishing
2544 Clinton Street
Buffalo, NY 14224

Copyright © 2025 Enslow Publishing

Designer: Tanya Dellaccio Keeney
Editor: Theresa Emminizer

Photo credits: Series art (notebook) Design PRESENT/Shutterstock.com; series art (stickers) tmn art/Shutterstock.com; cover (girl) Jihan Nafiaa Zahri/Shutterstock.com; p. 5 stockfour/Shutterstock.com; p. 7 tomeqs/Shutterstock.com; p. 9 mtmphoto/Shutterstock.com; p. 11 Veja/Shutterstock.com; p. 13 Prostock-studio/Shutterstock.com; pp. 15, 17 Lopolo/Shutterstock.com; p. 19 fizkes/Shutterstock.com; p. 21 Guaraciaba Seckler/Shutterstock.com.

Printed in the United States of America

Some of the images in this book illustrate individuals who are models. The depictions do not imply actual situations or events.

CPSIA compliance information: Batch #CSENS25: For further information contact Enslow Publishing, at 1-800-398-2504.

Find us on

CONTENTS

BOLDFACE WORDS APPEAR IN WORDS TO KNOW.

SPEAK UP!

Your feelings, thoughts, and ideas matter. Sometimes it can feel scary to use your voice. It can be hard to ask for help. It can be hard to share your feelings or stand up for yourself. Be brave! Your voice matters.

4

USE YOUR VOICE, EVEN IF IT SHAKES!

5

FEELING TONGUE-TIED

Something was bothering Rose. A kid at school hurt her friend. Rose knew she should speak up. But she was scared. She didn't know what to say. Staying quiet felt safer. But it hurt too. Rose felt all alone.

KEEPING YOUR FEELINGS INSIDE CAN BE LONELY.

7

FIND A SAFE LISTENER

If you have trouble using your voice, it can help to practice with someone you trust. Find an adult who makes you feel safe. Share the **situation** with them. Come up with some ideas together of things you could say or do.

PRACTICE USING YOUR VOICE BY **ROLE-PLAYING** WITH SOMEONE YOU TRUST.

9

WHEN TEASING ISN'T FUN

Aaron was mad. Steve kept **teasing** him because he didn't like scary movies. "You're such a baby!" Steve said. Steve tried to make Aaron watch scary movies. Aaron didn't like it. But Steve was his friend. What could Aaron do?

STEVE THOUGHT TEASING AARON WAS FUNNY. IT WASN'T!

11

PEER PRESSURE

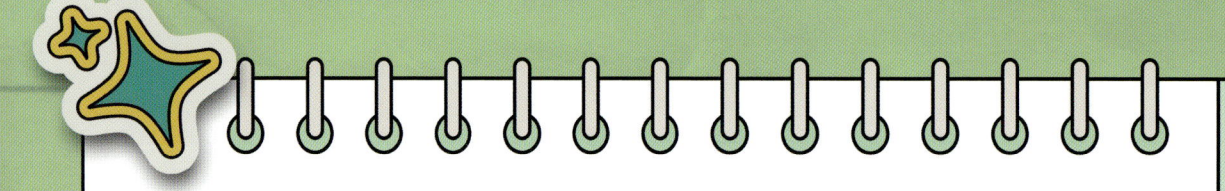

Sometimes we feel pressured, or pushed, by friends to do something or act a certain way. That's called peer pressure, and it isn't fun! Good friends don't pressure or force you. They respect your "no." If someone is pressuring you, use your voice!

PEER PRESSURE DOESN'T FEEL GOOD.

TRUTH OR DARE

Tina's friends were playing truth or dare. The dares kept getting wilder. Everyone was laughing. But Tina felt **uncomfortable**. She didn't want to **spoil** the fun, but she didn't want to play. Finally, Tina said, "I want to play something else."

TINA WAS BRAVE.
SHE STOOD UP FOR HERSELF!

15

EMPOWERMENT

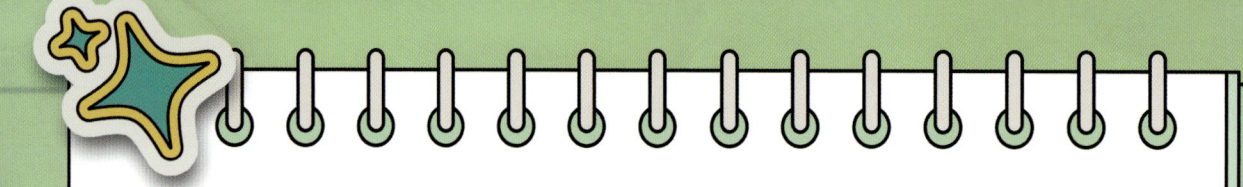

When you use your voice, you **empower** yourself. You empower others too! Maybe some of Tina's other friends were just as uncomfortable as she was. But they were too scared to speak up! When Tina spoke up, she empowered her friends to do the same.

16

WHEN WE TELL THE TRUTH WE HELP OURSELVES AND OTHERS.

17

GROWN-UPS SHOULD LISTEN

It's important to use your voice with grown-ups too! Safe adults will never force you to do something that makes you uncomfortable. Adults should never ask you to keep secrets. If an adult makes you feel unsafe, tell someone in your **safety circle**.

SAFE ADULTS WON'T DISMISS YOUR FEELINGS. THEY'LL LISTEN AND HELP!

19

TRUST YOURSELF

Listen to your feelings. If something feels wrong or makes you uncomfortable, don't **ignore** it. Use your voice and tell the truth about how you feel! If you say "no" and someone doesn't listen, talk to a safe adult right away.

YOUR VOICE MATTERS!

21

WORDS TO KNOW

dismiss: To act like something is unimportant.

empower: To give power or strength to someone.

ignore: To pretend something isn't happening.

role-playing: Playing pretend or acting something out.

safety circle: A group of three to five safe adults you can tell the truth to.

situation: A set of circumstances.

spoil: To ruin or mess something up.

teasing: Bothering or making fun of someone.

uncomfortable: Feeling unhappy or unsure.

22

FOR MORE INFORMATION

BOOKS

Harasymiw, Therese. *Are You Being Bullied?* New York, NY: PowerKids Press, 2021.

McAneney, Caitie. *I Talk to Cope.* New York, NY: PowerKids Press, 2023.

WEBSITES

Kids Health

kidshealth.org/en/kids/peer-pressure.html
Learn more ways to stand up to peer pressure.

Stop Bullying

www.stopbullying.gov/kids/what-you-can-do
Learn what you can do about bullying.

INDEX

24